CALLED UNTO HOLINESS

CALLED UNTO HOLINESS

By

RUTH PAXSON

Author of *Life on the Highest Plane,*
Rivers of Living Water, etc.

FOREWORD BY

REV. T. GEAR WILLETT

"For God hath not called us unto uncleanness,
but unto holiness" (I Thess. 4:7).

MOODY PRESS

CHICAGO

Printed in the United States of America

FOREWORD

It has been my privilege for many years to pray daily for the author of this book as one of the Lord's messengers, and I count it an added privilege to commend the record of these addresses to fellow believers everywhere. Some years ago, when associated with Miss Paxson at the Pei Tai Ho Convention in North China, it was with joy that one listened to messages marked with real clarity of thought and depth of spiritual teaching. Since then there has been an inward longing that opportunity might be given in England for a larger circle to be reached and this year has seen the fulfillment of this desire at Keswick Convention.

It is not the author's thought that every utterance of hers may be of sufficient value to be stereotyped in print, but yielding to the request of publishers and a number of friends these are to be issued in popular form as a companion volume to the one now so well known, *Rivers of Living Water*. The addresses are printed as delivered at the three meetings for ladies only and at the closing fellowship gathering and this will account for the more or less conversational style and freedom of approach.

There were many who prayed that this year's Keswick Convention would lead deeper into the truths of Scripture and the testimony of not a few is that these talks mark a part of the answer to those prayers.

That God may use this book to reveal to many of His servants the riches that there are in Christ Jesus and then by His Spirit to appropriate them for personal use will be my heartfelt prayer. In the words of a Chinese, great as an intercessor, "No one can do better than to study the Word of God devotionally and then pray it into the life."

T. GEAR WILLETT.

C.I.M.,
    London.
       September, 1936.

CONTENTS

ONENESS WITH CHRIST

I

ONENESS WITH CHRIST

From the Convention invitation that went out I read, "The dominant note of the messages will be a call to holiness of life—'Ye shall be holy, for I am holy.'" Do you want to be holy? Perhaps some of us here are defeated; we want to be victorious. We are enslaved; we want to be delivered. We are spiritually tired; we want rest. We are discouraged; we want peace. We are sorrowful; we want joy. But do we have a sense of the utter uncleanness of our lives, so that the deepest cry of our heart is for holiness?

Let us be honest. We must have come to Keswick for something. We must have come because we have a consciousness of some real need. But what is it that we want? Do we want to be holy? That is what God wants for us more than anything else. He wants us to be victorious, to be delivered, to be restful, to be joyous, and He has made provision for every one of these blessings for us in the Lord Jesus Christ. But above everything else in this world, He wants us to be holy. How do we share that desire of our Lord?

The twin word for holiness in Scripture is that precious word sanctification. Let us listen to what God says regarding His will and His calling for us.

> "For this is *the will of God*, even your *sanctification*" (I Thess. 4:3).

> "For God hath not *called* us unto uncleanness, but *unto holiness*" (I Thess. 4:7).

Christ prayed for our sanctification.

> "*Sanctify them* through thy truth; thy word is truth. For their sakes I sanctify myself, *that they also may be sanctified* through the truth" (John 17:17, 19).

It was the provision that God made in the gift of the Holy Spirit as our Sanctifier.

> "God hath from the beginning chosen you to salvation *through sanctification of the*

Spirit and belief of the truth" (II Thess. 2:13).

In Ephesians, where we have the deepest truths given us in all the Word of God regarding the relationship of the Christian to Christ, the favorite word for the Christian is "saint." Do you like to be called that? Every one of us is either a sinner or a saint in the sight of God. Perhaps it would make some of us very angry if someone called us a sinner. But would we resent it almost as much to be called a saint? We must be one or the other. It makes a tremendous demand upon you and me to be called a saint. But that is what the Lord, the Head of the Church, calls those who have been united to Him and have become part of His body.

Then, if we are saints, we certainly should live as saints. This was His purpose for us before there was ever a world or anyone in it.

"According as he hath chosen us in him before the foundation of the world, *that we should be holy*" (Eph. 1:4).

Think of it! "Before the foundation of the world" you, if you are in Christ, chosen to be holy, even as He is holy.

The truth of sanctification is as clearly taught in the Word of God as the truth of salvation. It is a glorious truth, and yet it is feared. It is a precious word, and yet it is shunned. There are two or three reasons for this. One is our ignorance of the meaning of it as God reveals it in His Book, so we are filled with prejudice. Another is unscriptural teaching about this glorious truth, and so we are filled with fear. Nowhere in the Word are we taught that sanctification means the eradication of the old sinful nature so that we are rendered impossible of sinning and even delivered from the presence of sin. Another reason is that scriptural sanctification makes too great a demand upon us, and so we resist the truth. We want a little leeway to sin left us. We do not truly desire to be holy.

What is the scriptural meaning of the word? The primary meaning is, someone or something wholly set apart unto God. Is not that beautiful?

If we are Christians at all, is not that what we want: to be wholly set apart unto God; to be separated unto the perfect possession, the complete control and the exclusive use of the Lord Jesus Christ is the primary meaning of the word "sanctified."

Then there is the secondary meaning: that which belongs to God must be like God. We must be holy for He is holy. God, the Holy Father; God, the Holy Son; and God, the Holy Spirit indwell the Christian. Is not that reason enough why we should be sanctified? Wholly set apart unto God? Made holy even as God Himself is holy?

But is such sanctification, issuing in holiness of life, the standard of the present-day church? Do we hear much about such a standard as this in the church today? Has each of us as a Christian taken such a standard? Far from it. On the contrary, we find such a lowered standard of life even among God's people. Someone, who taught a Bible class, asked for a definition of sin. One person in the class said, "That is very difficult to give today, because what we called sin twenty-five years ago we do not call sin today." Alas, that is only too true! There are Christian women wearing clothes today that twenty-five years ago would have been considered indecent. A minister's wife spoke to an unsaved woman asking her to accept Christ as her Saviour. The woman replied, "I do not wish to become a Christian, but if I were one, I would never appear in the house of God with such clothes as you wear." This lowered standard of life is the reason for the condition of the church today.

We find also a mixed standard in the church. There are people who are militantly orthodox in belief who are equally heterodox in conduct. I know one Christian woman who would not go to hear the pastor of her church preach—she would go to the Sunday school and then go home —because he was so modernistic. But she sent her little daughter to a dancing school. I know another woman who believes in the truth of the Bible from Genesis to Revelation and she has a certain standard for her life. She will not go to the cinema and she will not dance, but she smokes. The mixed standards among even orthodox Christians is another reason for the lack of holiness and power in the present-day church.

So we must turn to the Word and to the Lord to get our standard of what the Christian life is in the purpose of God. Let us listen to the words of our Lord in His last conversation with His disciples before His crucifixion.

> "I am the vine, ye are the branches: He that abideth in me, and I in him, the same bringeth forth much fruit: for without me ye can do nothing" (John 15:5).

The close, intimate nature of the Christian's relationship to Christ is revealed in the words, "I am the vine, ye are the branches." Within this relationship a threefold standard of life is revealed.

> "Ye in me"   —Oneness in Christ.
>
> "I in you"   —Likeness to Christ.
>
> "Much fruit"   —Fullness of Christ.

We are to have three messages at these meetings for women and they are to be on this threefold theme; oneness with Christ through positional sanctification; likeness to Christ through progressive sanctification; and fullness in Christ through personal sanctification.

Oneness with Christ through Positional Sanctification

"He that *abideth in Me*" (John 15:5).

That little word *"in"* is the biggest little word in all the Bible. Usually our first concern in our Christian experience is *what* we are. But *where* we are is of paramount importance, because where we are determines what we are. "Ye in me" precedes "I in you." The branch must be in the vine before it can bear fruit. Then, where are you today, my friend?

Two Trinities

The Bible shows us just two positions in which any human being can be—one is the position of the sinner, the other is that of the saint. To become a Christian we have to pass out of one position into the other. These two positions are radically different.

Scripture reveals with crystal clearness these two trinities as pictured, which we will now study together for a moment.

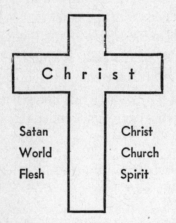

Christ

Satan	Christ
World	Church
Flesh	Spirit

Satan. Satan has a kingdom. Christ says so. In one passage recording the words of our Lord, the kingdom of God and the kingdom of Satan are put in exact antithesis to each other. Satan is the head of a rebel kingdom that was set up against the real kingdom of God. He is a traitor purposing to take God's place in the governmental affairs of the universe and in the worship of human hearts. He is "the prince of this world" and "the god of this age." He is the enemy of Christ and the adversary of the Christian.

The World. The world is the antithesis of the church. The best definition of the church is that given to us in the Epistle to the Ephesians where it is revealed as the body of Christ. Then what is the world? It is the body of Satan. It is human society without Christ. It is unregenerated mankind in captivity to and under the control of Satan.

"The whole world *lieth in* the wicked one" (I John 5:19, R.V.).

The position of the world is clearly stated. It is in Satan.

The Flesh. The flesh is all that one is without Christ. He has only a sinful nature that originated in Satan and entered into Adam as he yielded to the serpent's temptation in Eden. The flesh is the satanic spirit in the sinner.

Let us turn now to a moment's study of the other trinity.

Christ. He is the Head of God's kingdom, the One to whom all power in heaven and on earth has been given. Christ is the Saviour of the world who has been exalted to be Lord over the universe and Head over all things to the church. Christ is the Servant of God and the Saviour of men.

The Church. Have you thought of the church as the local church to which you belong? Sometimes I am asked if I belong to "*the* Church?" I come from the United States where we do not have a State Church and, of course, every one there believes that the denomination of which he is a member is *the* church. Well, what is *the* church? There is but one.

> "Gave him to be the head over all things to *the church, which is his body,* the fullness of him that filleth all in all" (Eph. 1:22, 23).

The church is a divine society in Christ. It is regenerated mankind in the possession, control and use of the Lord Jesus Christ.

The Spirit. The Spirit is the Holy Spirit. He is the very same Spirit who indwelt, infilled and empowered Christ, when He lived and worked on earth. On the day of Pentecost He was sent to indwell, infill and empower each Christian who formed the church.

The Two Trinities Exact Opposites

These two trinities are the exact opposite of one another. Satan is the very embodiment of evil and hate. His names and works show this. He is "the wicked one," "the adversary," "the tempter," "a liar," "a murderer," "a deceiver." Everything that he is and does is a manifestation of hate toward Christ and the Christian.

The world partakes of the nature of Satan as Christ Himself says.

> "The world cannot hate you; but me *it hateth,* because I testify of it that *the works thereof are evil*" (John 7:7).

"If ye were of the world, the world would love his own: but because ye are not of the world, but I have chosen you out of the world, therefore *the world hateth you*" (John 15:19).

The flesh is both evil and irreconcilably hostile toward God.

"Because *the carnal mind is enmity against God*: for it is not subject to the law of God, neither indeed can be" (Rom. 8:7).

Everyone has within him a traitor to God. It is that awful sinful nature the very essence of which is hostility to God.

But to turn to the other trinity we find Christ the very embodiment of holiness and love. All His names and works show it. He is "the Holy One and Just"; "the Good Shepherd"; "the merciful and faithful High Priest," "the Bread of Life," "the Saviour of the world." Everything that He is and does is the manifestation of love toward God and toward man.

The church partakes of the nature of Christ

and He is living within it now through the power of the Holy Spirit to make it holy and loving as He is. He will one day present it unto Himself perfected in holiness and without blemish.

> "But we all . . . are *changed into the same image* from glory to glory, even as by the Spirit of the Lord" (II Cor. 3:18).

> "That he might present it to himself *a glorious church, not having spot, or wrinkle or any such thing;* but that it should be holy and without blemish" (Eph. 5:27).

The Spirit is the *Holy* Spirit who is revealed as the Spirit of love in all His manifold operations.

Two Pictures

There are two pictures before us. One is the picture of a Satan-controlled, a world-conformed and a flesh-centered life. The other is the picture of a Christ-controlled; Christ-conformed; Christ-centered life. And they are pictures in color. One is in unrelieved midnight darkness that indicates the uttermost of ruin resulting in eternal death. The other is in unshadowed midday light that promises the uttermost of redemption resulting in eternal life.

Dear friend, in which of these trinities are you? You are in one or the other for there is no other place to be. There is no middle ground between these two positions. You are either in the trinity of which Satan is the head, of which the world is the embodiment, and the flesh is the expression; or you are in the trinity of which Christ is the Head, of which the church is the manifestation, and the Holy Spirit is the power. Where are you this moment? It is the most important question any human person ever faces in all his life. Will you not face it now and give your answer?

One thing, and only one thing, determines where you are. It is your relation to the crucified, risen, ascended, exalted Saviour and Lord. The salvation and the sanctification of the believing sinner required two outpourings—the outpouring of the blood of the Saviour on Calvary and the outpouring of the Spirit of the Lord at Pentecost.

The Blood of the Saviour

The blood of the Saviour is that which both saves and sanctifies.

> "Unto him that loved us, and washed us from our sins in his own blood" (Rev. 1:5).

> "Wherefore Jesus also, that he might sanctify the people with his own blood, suffered without the gate" (Heb. 13:12).

It is the blood alone that saves. Are you trusting for salvation in anything in yourself, in your character or in your good works? Or are you trusting in the sacraments or ordinances of the church? There is but one thing that saves and that is the blood of Jesus outpoured on Calvary's Cross.

It is the blood that sanctifies. It separated us from the kingdom of Satan. It crucified us unto the world and the world unto us. And it delivered us out of the sphere of the flesh.

The crucifixion of Jesus Christ put an end to the old creation and separated us completely from everything that pertains to it. It put aside everything *but Christ*. It placed Christ as Saviour at the very center of the Christian's life, making him Christ-centered.

The Baptism with the Spirit

Following Calvary came Pentecost. The believers in that upper room were baptized with the Holy Spirit, and the church, the body of Christ, was formed. Every believer came into oneness with Christ and with one another through that baptism. The fountain of fullness of life in Christ Jesus was opened and each one drank and was filled. From that day on down through the centuries every person who has put faith in the blood of the Saviour has been baptized by the Holy Spirit into that one body. He has been made one with Christ and the fullness of Christ's life has been made his *potentially*.

It is this Spirit-baptism that sanctifies. It separates us unto Christ, the church and the Spirit. It sets aside everything *unto Christ*. It puts Christ as the Life of our life and the Lord of our life, and makes the Christian Christ-conformed and Christ-controlled.

Now where are you? I want that question to be burned into every heart, so that if there is a single person here who is still living in that infernal trinity of midnight darkness of Satan, the world and the flesh, you will not be able to sleep until you have come out of it by putting simple faith in the blood of the Saviour.

The Cross of Christ—the Great Divide

The Cross of Christ is the Great Divide. It makes a clean-cut cleavage between the sphere of darkness and death and the sphere of light and life. It is the boundary line between the kingdom of Satan and the kingdom of God. It calls subjects out of the one kingdom into the other and compels the sinner to make a choice.

Have you responded to that call? Have you crossed that Great Divide? Have you put faith in the blood of your Saviour? The answer to this question determines not only with which trinity you choose to company in time, but with which you will spend eternity.

Perhaps the majority of us here in this place have chosen to come to Christ by way of the Cross. But, friends, we may think very lightly of the Cross of Christ. We can put a cross on top of a church building or hang it on the wall of our home, we can wear it as an ornament around the neck, we can place a cross as a bookmark in the Bible. But it is quite another thing to let the Cross of Christ make accursed everything in that old life, until it is impossible for us, knowingly and wilfully to give the devil place, or to be conformed to the world in any part of our life or to allow self still to have sovereignty over us.

The Baptism with the Spirit—The Open Fountain

As a Christian are you wholly set apart unto Christ ? Are you wholly in His possession, under His control and for His use? Will you frankly face this question today?

"Neither give place to the devil" (Eph. 4:27).

Have you given even standing room to the devil in your life? If so will you deliberately take it back now and yield that place to Christ?

"Be not conformed to this world" (Rom. 12:2).

Is your life at any point or in any phase conformed to the world? If you find any such conformity will you acknowledge it and come right out in complete separation at any cost?

"Put off the old man—Put on the new man" (Eph. 4:22, 24).

Will you honestly examine your life to see if you are under the dominion of the flesh at any known point? If so, will you deliberately "put off the old man" and "put on the new man"?

The question has been put on the negative side, let it now be put positively. Is Christ the source of everything in your life as far as you know? Is everything from Him? Is He the center of your life? Is everything in Him? Is He the goal of your life? Is everything for Him? That is the standard, my friends. Do not say that it is too high. I did not set such a standard for the

Christian's life. The Lord Jesus did it. But are not we Christians unutterably selfish if we want to get everything from Him for time and for eternity, and then give as little back to Him as we can? Are we willing to take this standard—Christ, the source of everything; Christ, the center of everything; Christ, the goal of everything, for our life?

That will cause us some heart searching. But for what did we come to Keswick? We shall not get the blessing we want in any easy way. There is no easy road to holiness. Are we willing to pay the price that we may have the prize? Christ is something to you, but is He *everything*?

There are three ways we can look upon Christ. We can say, "Yes, He is my Saviour, I could not get along without Christ. I would be unable to live and I surely would be afraid to die without Christ. I must have Christ, but I want Christ and——." Then after that word "and" we write in something out of that old trinity, that we still desire to keep and consider essential to our happiness. Christ is *not enough*. Christ does not satisfy altogether, so we go outside to get satisfaction in some worldly friendship or pleasure, or in some fleshly appetite or activity. Christ and——. Is that where some of us are in relationship to our Saviour? If it is, let us acknowledge it frankly.

I have a very dear Christian friend who is thoroughly orthodox. She honors the whole Word of God, and would loyally defend it against any attack. Christ is much to her but He is not yet everything. It is Christ and—the world, the cinema. Is it not a pity? We shall not have the cinema in heaven, thank God. We shall have to get along without it and many other things that seem tremendously necessary to us down here. Is the joy of heaven to be lessened for you because you will be compelled to leave the things of the world behind? But listen to what He says to us about the world here and now.

> "Love not the world, neither the things that are in the world. If any man love the world, the love of the Father is not in him" (I John 2:15).

Then there are others who say, "Yes, I must have Christ *but*——. He is my Saviour and I know He has perfectly cared for my past. But somehow He does not seem able to meet my present need. He is not sufficient for my circumstances, for my environment, for my sufferings and trials." Christ is *not equal* to my need. Christ does not suffice.

When I was in the United States not long ago I talked with a business woman who formerly had a good position and a fair bank account, and Christ as her Saviour. She got along very comfortably with the three. Then she lost both her position and her bank account. She came to me in great distress and depression. I said to her, "But you still have Christ, and He is equal to this difficulty and trial in your life." She said, "Yes. I have Christ *but*——," and lapsed back into her depression. For half an hour we talked, yet she did not get beyond "Christ *but*——." He was not equal to her difficulty, He did not suffice for her need. Oh! how wounded that all-sufficient One must have been!

But there is still another way in which we may look upon our Lord. Christ *only*; Christ *enough* to satisfy the affection and aspiration of the human heart. Christ only; Christ equal to every need of spirit, soul and body; to every demand of my circumstances and environment. Christ suffices for every trial and affliction and loss. Christ only, my all and in all. Can we say it? Is He that to you?

In closing, will you pardon a personal testimony to the all-sufficiency of Christ. I would give a good deal not to give it, but I dare not refuse to give it for this reason. Many times I have had people say, "It is very easy for you to be good for you have nothing to do but study your Bible and lead meetings." I often have the feeling when holding up any such standard of life as I have been this afternoon, that some people are thinking, "that is all right for her to say, but she is not in my situation, she does not have to live in my home with that cantankerous person with whom I live. She looks perfectly well and strong and does not have to endure the physical infirmity which I have. I know what she says is out of God's Word, but I do not believe it works in daily practical life."

May I testify to the unfailing sufficiency of the Lord Jesus Christ in severe affliction and great trial? Will you please do me the kindness of forgetting what I have to say of myself and remember only what is said of the all-sufficiency of Christ. For that purpose only is the testimony given.

I have been very ill for six weeks and have been out of bed only an hour or two a day until last Thursday, when for the first time I was up and dressed for a whole day. When the invitation came from Mr. Aldis several months ago to take these meetings, the Lord gave absolute assurance that the invitation came from Him and that it was His will to accept.

Then came a terrible attack of asthma which took me quickly to the lowest depths of physical suffering and weakness which, humanly speaking, made this ministry at Keswick seem quite impossible. But to me and to several close, praying friends, it seemed clearly an attack of Satan to thwart God in this ministry. Satan never wants a message given that reveals who he is and that magnifies the blood of the Saviour. But the temptation of Satan always has another side; it is the testing of God. When we realize that we can go right through, for our Lord Jesus is all-sufficient.

Last Thursday I hardly had breath enough to answer a question. For weeks it had been that way. But I said, "I will take Christ as my breath." I did, and He sufficed. My very life seemed ebbing away, and I thought "Christ is my life." And He was. Then my strength went down to the place where it seemed as though I had not enough strength to breathe another breath or even to offer a prayer. But I remembered the Word said that He is our strength. I took Him at His Word and He was my strength. But the most wicked work of Satan was attempting to rob me of a singing heart. You know the verse in Ephesians, "Singing and making melody in your heart to the Lord." What is the use of having breath, or life, or strength, if one has not a singing heart? So I said, "I will take Christ as my song," and He sufficed for the darkest hour.

Again and again in the night as I fairly fought for breath, the words came back to me, "Christ *is* all and *in* all," and, when He is that to one, He is all-sufficient. And I knew that if He were that to me, He would let me give this message to you.

Will you just take this testimony born out of trial and temptation? Will you believe that Christ is all-sufficient? If there is someone here who is struggling against some great trial in your physical life, your home circumstances, your spiritual experience, will you believe that Christ is enough and equal to it all? Will you let Him become all and in all to you?

Just this last word. It will mean a stripping of all that is not Christ. Are you willing for that in order that Christ may be pre-eminent in all things in your life and that you may be holy even as He is holy? Unto such a life have you and I been called.

LIKENESS TO CHRIST

II

LIKENESS TO CHRIST

The essential thing for holiness of life is to have a standard, and then to live without deviation by that standard. The Lord Jesus Christ has set that standard for us.

> "I am the vine, ye are the branches; he that abideth in me, and I in him, the same bringeth forth much fruit; for without me ye can do nothing" (John 15:5).

There is a threefold thing that He shows us here; oneness in Christ, likeness to Christ, the fullness of Christ. We thought together yesterday of oneness in Christ through our positional sanctification.

The sinner is living in that black, infernal trinity; Satan, the world, and the flesh. The Christian has passed by way of the Cross through faith in the atoning blood of the Saviour into a totally new position, a totally new sphere, a totally new trinity. He is in Christ, in the church, and in the Spirit, and thence he is called by God a saint. He has been made one with Jesus Christ through the baptism of the Holy Spirit by which he was brought into the body of Christ.

We said yesterday the most important question that can ever be put to a human being is this: Where are you? You are either in that black, infernal trinity over which Satan presides, or you are in that glory-lighted trinity over which Christ rules.

If you are still in Satan's trinity, are you going to remain there? Oh, that this afternoon there might be someone—if there is a single one who is not in Christ Jesus—who would put faith in the blood of the Saviour, for that is all that is necessary, and the moment you do it, you become a part of Him, and He becomes a part of you—oneness in Christ through positional sanctification.

Where we are determines *what* we are. So that is the question with which we come this afternoon: What are you now that you are in Christ.

Likeness to Christ through Progressive Sanctification

This thought takes us again to John 15, with which we are all so familiar. Oneness in Christ demands likeness to Christ; the branch that is in the vine must bear fruit. The branch that bears no fruit is worthless and is taken away.

> "Every branch in me that *beareth not fruit he taketh away*" (John 15:2).

What a solemn thought that is for every one of us who is a branch.

The second thought is that no branch can bear fruit of itself. There is absolutely nothing in the branch itself that is productive of fruit, nothing that the branch is, nothing that the branch can do, can make it produce fruit; only the sap of the vine produces fruit. So the branch has nothing to do but to abide in the vine.

"Abide in me, and I in you. As *the branch
cannot bear fruit of itself*, except it abide in
the vine; no more can ye, except ye abide in
me" (John 15:4).

Third, fruit-bearing is progressive. These verses
speak of the branch that bears "not fruit," the
branch that bears "fruit," the branch that bears
"more fruit," and the branch that bears "much
fruit."

"Every branch in me that beareth *not fruit*
he taketh away: and every branch that
beareth *fruit*, he purgeth it, that it may bring
forth *more fruit*" (John 15:2).

"Herein is my Father glorified, that ye bear
much fruit; so shall ye be my disciples"
(John 15:8).

There is nothing static in spiritual experience;
every real Christian is a growing Christian. The
purpose of fruit-bearing is to glorify Christ. The
branch does not bear fruit to glorify itself, it bears
fruit to glorify the vine. But only the "much
fruit" glorifies the Father. Anything short of

that, although it may bring Him joy and please Him, fails to glorify the Father fully.

Now what is fruit? It is Christ in His outward manifestation.

"*I in you. I in him*" (John 15:4).

Those words are so simple, you and I could read them over many times yet never sound the depths of their meaning. We could perhaps turn to this chapter and say, "I do not need to read those words, for I know them." So simple, yet the whole of Christian living is in these three words, "I in you." But if you were to underline one of these words, which would it be, the "you" or the "I"? The trouble is, we mark the "you," and the "you" is nothing and the "I" is everything. Only when that "you" becomes a zero, literally a zero, and the "I," even Christ Himself, fills the zero until only the "I" is seen, can we call ourselves real Christians according to the standard set in John 15, "I in you"—you nothing but a house of which the Lord Jesus Christ has taken possession, control and use.

Christ Himself is our Sanctification.

"But of him are ye in *Christ Jesus*, who of God is *made unto us* . . . sanctification" (I Cor. 1:30).

Christ Himself is our life.

"When *Christ, who is our life*, shall appear, then shall ye also appear with him in glory" (Col. 3:4).

The Christian life is not merely a converted life, it is not merely a consecrated life, it is not a Christian life at all unless it is a Christ-life.

It could not be more plainly illustrated than by my little wrist watch. You see it is a very tiny thing, and a very simple watch. It is not studded with jewels, that is not necessary for a watch. There is only one thing that a watch is really for; a watch is not an ornament, a watch is to keep time. That little watch would not be a bit of use to me if it did not keep time, for I have to catch trains and boats and attend meetings. The one thing I require in a watch is that it keeps time, and what makes it keep time? Its size? What it is made of, gold or silver? Not at all. It is the works that are inside.

What is a Christian for? Is he an ornament? A Christian has only one value in this world— to reveal Jesus Christ, to manifest Jesus Christ in this dark, sinful world where men do not know Him and do not read the Bible to find Him there. A Christian is an absolutely worthless Christian unless he is revealing Jesus Christ. What enables him to reveal Christ? Anything in himself? Nothing but the One that lives within him, the Lord Jesus Christ—"I in you." It is all that He asks of you and me, to let Him do the living and revealing.

He not only taught likeness through oneness, He prayed for it. Do you recall the last three words of His High-Priestly prayer? "I in them." The last words He wanted that little group, composed mostly of unlettered fishermen, to hear, so they would ring on in their ears and in their hearts and be unforgettable, were, "I in them." And, when He offered that petition, I believe He breathed out the deepest desire of His heart for every Christian all down through the ages. "I in them."

Has that prayer been answered in your life and mine, so that as we move in and out among people we are not seen, but only that living, glorious Christ is seen in us?

Now, we say that is too high a standard. Yes, it is a high standard, and do you know what we are constantly doing? We are appealing to Christ to look on our circumstances, our environment, to look at our weakness and our infirmity, and to bring His standard down to the level of our experience, and, friends, He will never do it. He has brought us to Keswick for the one purpose of bringing our experience up to the level of His standard. Are we going to let Him do it?

The other day I was talking with a man who said to me, "I am not a religious man, I am a pagan." Then he went on to speak of some divinity students he knew who went out to preach in the morning, and then came back and played poker and drank whiskey in the afternoon, and he said, "It does not seem quite right to me; a Christian ought to be Christlike."

That man said of himself that he was a pagan,

but he had a standard for the Christian that those Christians did not have for themselves. The world looks on at you and me, my friends, and if we profess to be a Christian, it says, "She ought to be Christlike," and she *ought* to be, or else make no profession of being a Christian, for the honor of His name.

Fruit is Christ in us manifested in His glory. But there are so many Christians one can only describe as drab, and I do not like drab. Do you? You do not like a drab Christian, either. We all like to see a glory-Christian. Are you one?

Fruit is Christ in us manifested in the glory of holiness. Now let us bring these two great truths together; Oneness in Christ—"Ye in me," and likeness to Christ—"I in you." The two are indivisible and inseparable. Oneness in Christ demands likeness to Christ. Fruit is Christlikeness, and much fruit is the fullest measure of Christlikeness; and Christlikeness is Christ in you, and Christ in you is manifested glory. Are you in Christ? Then *what* are you? Are you *like* Christ? Are you bearing fruit? Can others see

Christ in you? To what measure are you bearing fruit? Only fruit, or more fruit, or much fruit? Would the members of your family know you are a Christian if you did not go to church? Would your friends know that you are a Christian if you did not testify or pray? Would any one know it if he just looked into your face?

Friends, it ought to be seen. If Christ lives in us, there should be something in the expression of the eye, something in the very lines of the face; we should bear the mark in our faces of the presence of the glorified Christ within. Would one know it from our conversation or from watching our daily walk? When you enter a room, do you cast a chill over the atmosphere, or do you flood it with sunshine? A glory-Christian will flood every place he goes with sunshine, the sunshine of the presence of the glorified Christ. Is Christ the very life of your life?

I am sure that we all want to be Christians who are bearing much fruit, who flood every place we go with the sunshine of His presence. Some of us came to Keswick for the very purpose of finding out how to live such a life. How, then, may we live it? Likeness to Christ through progressive sanctification requires two things of us; first, a right relationship to Christ, our Sanctification, and secondly, a right adjustment to the Holy Spirit, our Sanctifier.

A Right Relationship to Christ

To be like Christ requires that we come into a full relationship to the Lord Jesus Christ. It is not enough just to accept Him as Saviour. That is taking simply the first step. We must go on to let Christ become the Life of our life, and above all to let Him be Lord of our life. We read in Romans 5 of three things that sin did. Sin entered, sin abounded, sin reigned. Sin reigned. Do you get the full force of the word "reigned"? Sin was absolute dictator over your life and mine; sin possessed us, sin controlled us, sin used us.

But now Christ is our Saviour and we are in Him. Is sin still to reign over us? Are we to continue to live in sin? Inconceivable! Who but One has the right to reign, the One who has been made Head over all things to the Church and to the Christian? Christ now has the right to possess us fully, to control us completely and to use us exclusively. In order that He may do so, He must become Lord. But sin, that stubborn old ruler, will contest His claim every step of the way. But did God make provision for the dethronement of that old master sin?

> "Knowing this, that *our old man is crucified with him*, that the body of sin might be destroyed, that henceforth we should not serve sin" (Rom. 6:6).

What does that word "destroyed" mean? To be rendered inoperative. In modern terms, to be put out of employment, out of a job as ruler over your life. And for what purpose is this dethronement? "That we might no longer" serve sin. We have a new Master, even the Lord Jesus, and Him only are we to serve now.

A Choice between Sovereigns

You and I are called to make a choice of sovereigns. As a sinner we had to choose between our sins and our Saviour, now as a Christian we must make the choice between the continued sovereignty of that old master, Sin, and that of our new master, Christ.

> "*Let not sin therefore reign* in your mortal body, that ye should obey it in the lusts thereof" (Rom. 6:12).

Have you made this choice? Has it been a deliberate, final choice of Christ as the sole Sovereign over your life? If not, will you do it this afternoon?

Christ Yielded to as Lord

Having chosen Christ as our Master, then He commands us to yield to Him as Lord.

> "Neither yield ye your members as instruments of unrighteousness unto sin: but *yield yourselves unto God*, as those that are alive from the dead, and your members as instruments of righteousness unto God" (Rom. 6:13).

"*Yield yourselves*," spirit, soul and body. Yield your whole human personality *in toto* to Christ. Have you done it? Or have you parcelled out a little bit and told Him what He could have, and what you intended to reserve for yourself?

"Yield *your members*." In order that there may be no loophole, He goes on to say we are to yield every member of the body—the eyes, the ears, the feet, the hands, the lips, the tongue. Have you done it? Perhaps someone here is living in defeat because of one unyielded member of the body. An unyielded tongue, what unlimited harm it can do! Here is our Lord's command, have we obeyed it? Have we yielded ourselves entirely to Him? If not, will you do it now?

Then we must yield everything that has any relationship whatsoever to our life, all our habits, all our practices, all our appetites, our pleasures, our companionships, our home, our possessions, our children, our money.

Last year, after a message on yielding, a gentleman came up to me and said, "Miss Paxson, tonight I have yielded my old pipe." Can you not see that old pipe? The Lord had asked him for it, perhaps many a time. He thought he had yielded it, but he took it home and put it up on the shelf. What he **ought** to have done with the old pipe was to have thrown it, with everything that appertained to it, into the fire. That is yielding; but, when he saw the old pipe, perhaps he was tempted to think, "May I not take down the old pipe just once again for one more puff?"

Have you yielded your old pipe? It may not be one you put in your mouth, but you may have a blood relation to it, that you do puff away at, which the Lord is asking you to yield. Oh! this is the shame of many even Christian women today! How can you distinguish a woman of the church, the body of Christ from a woman of the world, the body of Satan, if she is puffing a cigarette? What is there to mark her off as belonging to the glory-life?

What is your old pipe, my friend? I will tell you what it is. It is that thing the Lord has been asking you for, for weeks and months, maybe for years, and you will not give it up; that little insignificant thing that is not worth more than the puff of a pipe, and you will not give it

up for this eternal Son of God, that His glory
may be manifested more fully in you. That is
what He brought you here for, to get rid of that
old pipe. I do not know what it is, but He knows,
and you know. It is that which is keeping you in
defeat and it is that which is hindering Him from
manifesting His glory in your life today. Will
you yield that old pipe to the Lord Jesus Christ.
Will you yield yourself, your members, all that
you are and have, to the Lord now?

The Right Adjustment to the Holy Spirit

This work of sanctification can be carried on
only through the Holy Spirit, the Sanctifier, that
second great gift bestowed at the time of con-
version. The moment you were brought into
union with Christ, the wonderful Holy Spirit
came to indwell you, and He is there for one
purpose, to glorify Christ in you. How does He
do this?

The Spirit of Truth who Enlightens

As the Spirit of truth He enlightens us that
we may know what we possess in Christ and

what Christ possesses in us. Ephesians speaks of a double inheritance, the saint's inheritance in Christ and Christ's inheritance in the saint.

> "That the God of our Lord Jesus Christ, the Father of glory, may give unto you the Spirit of wisdom and revelation in the knowledge of him: *The eyes of your understanding being enlightened; that* ye *may know* what is the hope of his calling, and what the riches of the glory of his inheritance in the saints, and what is the exceeding greatness of his power to usward who believe" (Eph. 1:17-19).

The Spirit of truth gives us a progressive revelation of Christ and of our riches in Him so, that once having seen Him we will want Him and Him only.

The Spirit of Power who Enables

As the Spirit of power He enables us that we may possess what we know to be ours in Christ. He is the power that worketh in us to make

Christ a living reality within and to fill us unto all the fullness of God.

> "That he would grant you, according to the riches of his glory, to be *strengthened with might by his Spirit in the inner man,* that Christ may dwell in your hearts by faith; . . . that ye might be filled unto all the fullness of God" (Eph. 3:16, 17, 19).

The Spirit of power works for a progressive realization of Christ within us as our Life and our Lord.

The Spirit of Holiness who Separates

As the Spirit of holiness He separates us from the world. He shows us there can be no mixture between darkness and light, no friendship between the world and the church. The Spirit makes us know that whoever is a friend of the world is in the sight of God an adulteress for that one has broken the marriage vow to Christ, and by so doing has become the enemy of God.

> "*Be ye not unequally yoked together with unbelievers:* for what fellowship hath right-

eousness with unrighteousness? and what communion hath light with darkness? Wherefore *come out from among them*, and *be ye separate*, saith the Lord" (II Cor. 6: 14, 17).

"*Ye adulteresses* (who break your marriage vow to Christ), know ye not that *the friendship of the world is enmity with God?* Whosoever therefore would be a friend of the world maketh himself an enemy of God" (James 4:4, R.V.).

The Spirit of holiness works progressively to separate us from earthly things and from the love of the world and to strip us of everything of which Christ is not the source, the center and the goal.

The Spirit of Life who Counteracts

As the Spirit of life He counteracts all the work of the flesh within. While the Christian is no longer in the flesh, the flesh is still in him and remains there through life. The flesh will do everything it can possibly do to regain possession, control and use of the life. But that wonderful Spirit of life is within to counteract all the workings of the flesh, and, when we let the Holy Spirit have absolute control, He can keep the flesh from having dominion and power over us.

> "For the law of *the Spirit of life* in Christ Jesus *hath made me free* from the law of sin and death" (Rom. 8:2).

> "For the flesh lusteth against the Spirit, and *the Spirit against the flesh*; and these are contrary the one to the other; so that ye cannot do the things that ye would" (Gal. 5:17).

The Spirit of life works progressively to counteract the flesh by taking control and by crowning Christ Lord of all in life and work.

The Spirit of Glory who Conforms

As the Spirit of glory He conforms us to the image of the Lord Jesus Christ. As He frees us from the earthly, He fashions us into the heavenly.

"But we all, with unveiled face beholding as in a mirror the glory of the Lord, are *transformed into the same image from glory to glory,* even as from the Lord the Spirit" (II Cor. 3:18, R.V.).

What a picture in promise of our progressive sanctification! Today like Christ, but tomorrow we may be still more like Christ; every day may see some new touch of glory added to the life and some new bit of likeness to Him may be revealed to those with whom we live and work. The Spirit of glory works progressively to conform us to the image of Christ *from glory to glory* so that we may grow up into Him in all things.

And what is the result of the work of the Holy Spirit, our Sanctifier?

Realized Holiness of Life

We become the Christian who bears the much fruit.

"But *the fruit of the Spirit* is love, joy, peace, longsuffering, gentleness, goodness, faith, meekness, temperance (self-control)" (Gal. 5:22, 23).

A wonderful cluster of fruit that cannot be broken! Nine marvelous, heavenly, spiritual graces that reveal to us the perfection of the moral character of Jesus Christ. And they are to be in us as the work of this divine Spirit in beautiful symmetry and in ever-growing evidence of the life of Christ within.

But how often we see a life that has one of these characteristics in a marvelous way but sadly lacks in another and the testimony of the life is marred thereby. At a meeting once in China, a Chinese doctor was translating for me. She was the largest Chinese woman I ever saw and her heart of love was as big as her body. But in the midst of the message which had brought conviction to her own soul, she stopped me and confessed to the nurses, who worked under her supervision, the sin of so often losing her temper. She had love but not self-control.

Sometimes you will see a Christian who truly bears great trial and affliction with long-suffering, but she has a face as long as her long-suffering. There is long-suffering, but no joy.

Then again you will meet someone who is the soul of goodness, but her face is a mass of wrinkles, made by fretting and worry. There is goodness but no peace.

A while ago after speaking at a meeting a woman came up and introduced herself. She immediately began talking about herself. Within two minutes she made this astounding statement, "I hope you will not think me boastful, but everything I do is a success." Well, I did not want to misjudge her, but it did sound a bit boastful. She continued the conversation about herself and soon had made this same remark again. She was a woman of faith, quite orthodox in fact, but seemed lacking in meekness. The only memory I have of that Christian woman is that boastful remark. It set me thinking. What do people think of the last remark they heard me make? What memories do I leave behind me? It is a solemn thought. Have we drawn attention to ourselves, or have we fixed the thought of others upon our glorified Lord? Is there anything in you or in me that is worth the slightest thing? Should not our Lord have all the glory in everything?

Are we the much-fruit bearing Christians? Do we manifest His love, joy, peace, long-suffering, gentleness, goodness, faith, meekness and self-control in ever-increasing beauty and symmetry?

FULLNESS OF CHRIST

III

FULLNESS OF CHRIST

We have been considering together in these meetings the standard which the Lord Jesus Christ set for the Christian as given in that last conversation with His disciples on earth. It was to be a life like His life. They were to live as He had lived, and to work as He had worked. In other words they were to live a supernatural life. But how was such a life possible for human, sinful men?

In the definition of the church given in the Epistle to the Ephesians we see the same high standard set.

> "The church, which is his body, the fullness of him that filleth all in all" (Eph. 1:22,23).

Think of it! "The church, the fullness of Christ"! The Christian, the fullness of Christ! Is that your conception of what it is for you to be a

Christian. You, living in your home; you, walking up and down the streets of your town or city, the fullness of Christ! That is what the Word says. "The fullness of *him who filleth* all in all." Here we are told how it is possible. He fills us with His own fullness.

But, as He set this standard before His disciples on that last night with them, He saw their perplexed look and the sorrow in their faces. If they had not been able to live according to such a standard when He was with them, how could they possibly live such a life when He had gone from them. Then He told them how.

He was going away, but He would send Another like Himself to be not only with them but in them.

> "And I will pray the Father, and *he shall give you another Comforter*, that he may be with you for ever . . . for he dwelleth with you, and *shall be in you*" (John 14:16, 17).

The supernatural life could be lived because they were to be indwelt by a supernatural Person, whose indwelling Presence was for one purpose, to make the life of Christ a living reality within them.

He promised to send this wonderful Comforter, but, in order to do so, He must go away. Yes, He had to go to the Cross where He laid down that precious life in death. He had to go down into the darkness of the tomb but He could not be kept there. He, who was the Author of life, yea, who was Life itself, broke the bonds of death and rose from the tomb. He ascended into heaven and was exalted by the Father to be Lord over the universe and Head over all things to the Church. As the exalted, glorified Lord, He would send back the Holy Spirit, Who had indwelt, infilled and empowered Him in His earthly life, to indwell, infill and empower them.

The Fullness of Christ Through Personal Sanctification

The day of Pentecost came. The Holy Spirit descended and that little company of believers were baptized with the Holy Spirit and so made one in the body of Christ. Then they were all

filled with the Holy Spirit on this birthday of
the church.

"And they were *all filled with the Holy
Spirit*" (Acts 2:4).

By so doing Christ, the Head of the church,
set the standard for the entire church and for
every Christian all down through the ages. It is
not at the end of our Christian life in the twi-
light of Christian experience we are privileged to
be filled with the Spirit as a sign of spiritual
maturity. But at the very beginning, yea, on any
day after we have been baptized into the body of
Christ through rebirth, we may be filled with the
Holy Spirit as the means of becoming full-grown
in Christ.

My friends, to be filled with the Spirit is God's
standard for every Christian here this afternoon.
Are you filled? The only normal Christians here
are those who are filled with the Holy Spirit.
We sometimes think this is such an extraordinary
spiritual experience that the person, who is so
filled, is abnormal. It is the exact contrary.
I put it to you today, is it normal for one who

is in Christ and has Christ in him and who is indwelt by the same Spirit that indwelled Christ, to be constantly defeated? Is it normal for that one to be without joy, or peace, or rest, or power? Is it normal for the Christian to be simply bearing "fruit" when he should be bearing "much fruit"?

So I do not wait until the close of my message to press home this question. Are you filled with the Holy Spirit? We can know whether we are filled or not as truly as we can know whether or not we are saved. There are conditions to be fulfilled by us for receiving and conditions for maintaining the fullness of the Spirit which are as clearly stated in the Word as the conditions to be fulfilled for salvation. We may and should know what they are.

We shall think now of how to obtain this fullness. We shall do so by asking and answering questions from the Word of God.

Has Such Fullness Been Provided For Me?

Oneness in Christ made it ours.

> "For in him dwelleth all the fullness of the Godhead bodily, and *in him* ye are *made full*" (Col. 2:9, 10, R.V.).

"In him dwelleth all the fullness of the Godhead bodily." We all believe that, do we not? But we cannot stop there. It goes on to say, "And ye are made full in him." Our position in Christ makes us potential partakers of the fullness of Christ. We "are made full" it says, not we will be. The moment we become a part of the body of Christ, the fountain of fullness in Him is opened to us. The fullness has been provided for every Christian.

Is Such Fullness Possible For Me

Our theme today is "The Fullness of Christ through personal Sanctification." Can the fullness provided be made personal? Is it possible for me? Let the Lord Jesus give us the answer.

> "But whosoever drinketh of the water that I shall give him shall never thirst; but *the water that I shall give him shall be in him a well of water springing up into everlasting life*" (John 4:14).

"*Water*" in Scripture is the type of the Spirit as Christ Himself interprets it in John 7:38, 39. Christ is never called the water of life, but He gives this water to those who thirst and drink. Christ gives the Holy Spirit to the Christian. He is promising here the gift of the Holy Spirit.

"*In him a well*"—is the Holy Spirit indwelling which Christ promised the disciples.

"A well of water *springing up*"—leaping up in an exhaustless, irrepressible way; springing up and overflowing. Is not this fullness?

"*Whosoever*"—Did you get that word? It is big enough to include you if you want to be inside. Whenever I find a "whosoever" of promise from the lips of my Lord, I want to be inside as quickly as possible. Do you want to be inside this "whosoever"? You may be if you will. To whom were these words spoken? To the most respectable, cultured, educated, moral woman in that Samaritan city? The exact opposite. Perhaps to the most wicked woman there. Think of that! If you and I had been talking to that poor sinful woman we would have said to her

"Ye must be born again." And to Nicodemus, ruler of the Jews, the cultured, gifted, gentleman, we would have spoken of the living water. But not so with Jesus. He went no further in the conversation with Nicodemus than exhortation to be born again, while to the wicked woman He offered the gift of the fullness of the Spirit. It is for you, whoever you are, and for me, is it not, if we want it?

"Shall never thirst." Do you believe it? You know when Jesus says "never" He means "never." When you and I say "never" we usually mean "sometimes." But when Jesus said "never thirst" He meant "never thirst." And what do the words mean? Perfect inward heart satisfaction. Do you have it? Do you know many people who do? How many people do you see whose faces seem to show that their hearts are satisfied? My friends, if everyone of us women in this tent today had such a face, a revival should start immediately. It would indicate a quiet, peaceful, restful heart. And people would be asking how we got it.

After our first meeting someone said to me, "Did you see the person on the front seat with such a radiant face?" I was sorry to say I had not seen her. But in thinking of it afterwards it impressed me that it should be such an extraordinary thing, especially at a Keswick Convention, to see a radiant face that someone would remark about it. Why should not every Christian in that meeting have had such a radiant face that the one who had an unhappy face would have been the exception? Does this not seem abnormal and wrong?

"Whosoever drinketh of the water that I shall give him shall never thirst" but shall have perfect inward satisfaction and sufficiency. No matter what the circumstances or the environment or the spiritual and temporal need, Christ is enough and equal to it all. Christ only satisfies; Christ only suffices because the indwelling Holy Spirit fills the life and makes Christ a living reality within. Is He doing that for you?

I would hardly know how to answer anyone who asked me if I had been at the Keswick Convention. I have been in the town of Keswick but, because of my illness, sitting day after day in my room at the hotel, unable to go to any meetings or to receive the blessing that would come through personal fellowship with the speakers and friends here at Keswick. But have I not been at Keswick nevertheless? What is "Keswick"? Is it only a town? Is it only a giant tent? Is it only an enormous crowd? Is it only meetings from morning until night? The inwardness of that word "Keswick" is the presence of the living Lord as a living reality manifested through the power of the Holy Spirit indwelling the Christian. If you have not known that, then you have not been at Keswick at all, though you have attended every meeting. And I if I have known that, then I have been at Keswick though I have not been able to attend any other meetings than these. And, if we have experienced the presence of the living Christ in a larger measure than ever before through a fresh infilling of the Holy Spirit, then "Keswick" will go to the ends of the earth by the rivers of living water flowing through us.

You remember that Samaritan woman went to the well with a waterpot, but she left it there. There are some people who come to Keswick with a little waterpot to be filled with living water, hoping it would last until they could come to Keswick again. Did you do that? Oh! Leave your little waterpot here and go away knowing that you have a well of living water within you springing up into everlasting life. Then you can go back to the most drab, difficult circumstances in home, in business, or in social circle and carry Christ into every situation. That each of us may do if we drink of this living water until filled. It is not God's desire to give us merely a waterpot full of blessings, just victories, but rather, to give us a well, the fullness of Him who is the Blesser and the Victor.

Then, may I also have this fullness for power? For some of us are conscious of lack not only in the realm of Christian character but also in the sphere of our spiritual service. We have to acknowledge a lack of passion and of power to win souls to Christ. Let us listen again to the words of our Lord.

"If any man thirst, let him come unto me and drink. *He that believeth on me,* as the scripture hath said, *from within him shall flow rivers of living water*" (John 7:37, 38, R.V.).

"Rivers of living water"—not a rivulet, or stream, or even a river, but "rivers," the Amazon, the Mississippi, the Yangtze, the Thames, all put together into one.

"Shall flow"—not a Dead Sea that receives and retains the blessings of Keswick, but the river Jordan that refreshes and renews every life it touches. Rivers of living water flowing out of Keswick into every village, town, city and country represented here at Keswick, so that "everything shall live whither the river cometh."

Plenitude of power in the Spirit-filled church! When in the United States last year I passed through the mid-western states which had suffered so terribly from drought. The train crossed over a very long bridge beneath which was a very tiny stream of water twisting its way through a wide dried-up river bed. What a parable it was of many of our present-day churches! Expensive buildings, magnificent pipe-organs, big programs, countless organizations, something on almost every day of the week, yet so few souls saved and so few Christians filled with the Holy Spirit. Oh! why is it that with the church better organized and equipped than ever before in its history, it has so little power? What would it mean if from Keswick five thousand people went forth with rivers of living water flowing from the life? It would mean revival that would extend to the uttermost part of the earth.

Plenitude of power in each Spirit-filled Christian! A woman attending a conference in Holland last summer was filled with the Holy Spirit, and during the week of the conference, while she attended all the meetings, won four people to Christ. Two women went home filled with the Holy Spirit for the first time and within six weeks they had brought six other women to share that same wonderful experience. Will this happen in some lives here in Keswick?

"From within him"—an inflow demands an outflow and an overflow. Christ is enough and

to spare. And for whom is this plenitude of power?

"He that believeth on me"—not only for some great preacher or Bible teacher, not even alone for some one employed in Christian service, but for him who believes on the Lord Jesus Christ. Do you believe? Then this promise is for you. Not even the youngest, or the weakest or the least gifted believer is excluded from this blessing.

A missionary came home from China on furlough last year. On the boat she met a young woman who was unsaved but troubled over her spiritual condition. She sought help from the missionary and was open to know the way of salvation. But the missionary could not lead her to Christ. This caused desperate discouragement and led her to determine not to return to the mission field. Then a glorious thing happened. She was filled with the Holy Spirit and the Lord did such a gracious thing, so like Him. He brought that young woman across her path again and gave her the power to win her to Christ. Filled with the Holy Spirit, then able to win souls to Christ. Are you doing it? Are you able to do it? If you are filled with the Holy Spirit, then those rivers of living water will flow through you into other lives.

Is such Fullness Optional?

May I choose whether I will be filled with the Holy Spirit or not? The Bible answers that question.

"*Be ye filled* with the Spirit" (Eph. 5:18). It is a command. Christian friends, are you and I free to disobey the command of Christ? Or are we free to choose which commands we will obey and which we will not? I read in God's Word, "Thou shalt not kill." I find not one bit of difficulty in obeying fully that command, for I have never seen one human being I desired to kill. "Thou shalt not steal." This command also is easy to obey, for I have never seen anything I wanted badly enough to steal it and run the risk of going to prison. To obey this command presents little difficulty to me. But, "Be ye filled with the Spirit." "No, Lord, I do not want to be filled with the Holy Spirit for it makes too great a demand upon me. I will have to live too holy a life. I do not wish to obey this command." Can we say that to our Lord?

Here is a command, and obedience to it puts the Christian in possession of the greatest spiritual blessing possible this side of heaven. Then is not disobedience to this command the Christian's greatest sin? For if not filled with the Holy Spirit, it is impossible for him to live a life of victory, holiness and power. No, to be filled with the Holy Spirit is not optional but obligatory upon every Christian, and the Christian who is not so filled is sinning.

Why Do I not have The Fullness of the Spirit?

There are two objective causes in the realm of truth. One is ignorance. In Christ we possess the fullness of the Godhead, and in the Spirit we have the One who makes this fullness our personal possession. But, because of ignorance of the Word of God, we lack this knowledge. Consequently we lack the experience of fullness.

The other cause is unbelief. We know the truth but only intellectually and doctrinally. It has not become heart experience. Or we know it but we are afraid to act upon our knowledge and to appropriate this blessing by faith.

"So we see that they could not enter in because of unbelief" (Heb. 3:19).

Then there are two subjective causes in the realm of experience. One is unconfessed sin. The Holy Spirit is holy and the place He indwells must be made and kept holy. This infilling demands cleansing from all known sin. It is impossible to be filled with the Holy Spirit while knowingly, deliberately, retaining sin in the life.

The cleansing of the temple during the wonderful revival under King Hezekiah, as recorded in II Chronicles 29, shows us the manner and the extent of the cleansing God requires of us.

"Hear me, ye Levites, sanctify now yourselves, and sanctify the house of the Lord God of your fathers, and carry forth the filthiness out of the holy place" (II Chron. 29:5).

"And the priests *went into the inner* part of
the house of the Lord, *to cleanse it,* and
brought out all the uncleanness that they
found in the temple of the Lord" (II Chron.
29:16).

"Now they *began on the first day* of the
month to sanctify . . . and *in the sixteenth
day* of the first month they *made an end*"
(II Chron. 29:17).

Did you note the word "filthiness"? God uses
no soft, sentimental words when He talks about
sin. He calls it what it is, "filthiness." Filthiness
in "the holy place." How did so much uncleanness accumulate in the holy place that the king
was compelled to order a special cleansing of the
temple? Note, also, that they did not begin
cleansing at the *outer* court of the temple and
stop there but "they went into the *inner* part of
the house of the Lord to cleanse it." Note, too,
that they did not merely find the uncleanness
but they *brought it out* and they did not bring
out only some of the uncleanness but "*all* the
uncleanness that they *found.*" It was a most

thorough going house-cleaning. And how long did it take to do it? Exactly sixteen days. What a tremendous amount of filthiness to remove! But they persevered until it was done.

Now let us turn to the counterpart of this truth in the New Testament. We are struck by the similarity of the teaching even to the use of some of the same words.

> "Know ye not that ye are the temple of God, and that the Spirit of God dwelleth in you?
>
> If any man defile the temple of God, him shall God destroy; for the temple of God is holy, which temple ye are" (I Cor. 3:16, 17).
>
> "Let us cleanse ourselves from all filthiness of the flesh and spirit, perfecting holiness in the fear of God" (II Cor. 7:1).

"Ye the temple of God" which "temple is holy." Therefore it must be cleansed from all filthiness both of the flesh and of the spirit.

There may have been gross, vulgar, even sensuous sins in the life of the past. Perhaps we are rid of these grosser, fleshly sins, but what of those which still defile our innermost spirit? We used to lie. Now we would not tell a deliberate, out-and-out lie, but there is hypocrisy, deceit, double-dealing. Even in our Christian experience there is a profession of Christ which is not evidenced in our possession of Christ. Formerly we had a violent temper to which we gave way constantly. Now there is a large measure of control of outward bursts of temper. But what about that secret irritability and impatience in the spirit? Once we frankly and outspokenly hated someone and said so. To us now that is sin, but is there still lurking in some dark corner of the heart the jealousy or resentment that caused the hate? We would not now openly quarrel with someone as we once did, but if we see somebody we do not like, we just cross to the other side of the street. And we think we are victorious, spiritual Christians not needing cleansing.

One time in China I went to a girls' school to take a series of meetings. One of the missionaries came to me and said, "Do not ask me to do any personal work among the girls during these meetings, for I will not do it." She went on to say, "I am going home on furlough and I am not coming back. I have already told my missionary and Chinese co-workers that I cannot return because of the condition of my health." Her health was breaking down it is true. But the cause of the breakdown was not physical but spiritual. As she talked I was studying her face. There was a line in her forehead that ought not to have been there. As we go on growing into spiritual maturity there are some lines marking this growth of character that will be in our faces. But there are other lines that are the footprints of sin. And these two kinds of lines are distinguishable.

I began quoting verses on victory from the Bible. She could say every one of them by heart. I spoke of books on victory. She knew them all and had read many of them. The doctrine and phraseology of victory were very familiar to her but she did not have victory. You ask, "Did she have some great gross sin of the flesh that overwhelmed her?" Oh! no, it was nothing but a little hurt that she had allowed to sink down into the depths of her heart four years previously and which she had nursed until it had robbed her of her peace of heart, her joy in Bible study and prayer, and her passion for lost souls. More than that it had brought on her physical illness and was finally taking her home not to return to the mission field. A little hurt hidden away in a human heart doing damage like that! Is there anything of this kind deep down in your spirit? If so, will you cleanse yourself of it today? That dear missionary got rid of that hurt and has since been home on two furloughs and returned to China where she is today.

Last summer at a conference in Switzerland a grey-haired man made a public confession at the close of one meeting that for twenty-seven years he had had nothing to do with his relatives. For years he had suffered from insomnia. That night, after his confession and cleansing, he slept like a babe. On the following Lord's Day he testified that for twenty-seven years he had not known peace of heart as the last three days.

"*If we confess our sins*, he is faithful and just to forgive us our sins, *and* to cleanse us from all unrighteousness" (I John 1:9).

"He that covereth his sins shall not prosper; but *whoso confesseth* and *forsaketh them* shall have mercy" (Prov. 28:13).

It is utterly foolish and futile for any one of us to pray for the fullness of the Holy Spirit if we hold even so much as a tiny spark of known resentment, or hurt, or unlove, or any un-Christlike feeling toward another. We shall pray in vain. Are you willing to have all uncleanness, both of the flesh and of the spirit, carried out of your life?

The cleansing is not the infilling but it rids us of what prevents the fullness and makes us ready for it.

The second subjective cause for the lack of fullness is an unyielded life, which means an uncrucified and uncontrolled self. Infilling demands the yielding of ourselves *in toto* to the Lordship of Christ. It permits of no reservations;

it allows no locked doors. We must part with everything of which Christ is not the source and we must place everything under Christ's control. There must be the utter dethronement of self and the voluntary enthronement of Christ.

In the revival under Hezekiah we see, following the cleansing of the temple, the consecration of themselves and of their sacrifices and thank offerings.

> "Hezekiah said, Now ye have consecrated yourselves unto the Lord, come near and bring sacrifices and thank offerings into the house of the Lord. And the congregation brought in sacrifices and thank offerings: and as many as were of a free heart burnt offerings" (II Chron. 29:31).

After the filthiness was carried out the offerings were brought in.

Just so is the divine order in the cleansing and consecration of the Christian who is God's holy temple. The "perfecting of holiness" follows the cleansing from all the filthiness of the flesh and spirit. This comes by presenting the body to the Lord as a living sacrifice for His perfect possession, complete control, and exclusive use.

"I beseech you therefore, brethren, by the mercies of God, that *ye present your bodies a living sacrifice*, holy, acceptable unto God, which is your reasonable service" (Rom. 12:1).

"He died for all, that *they which live should not henceforth live unto themselves, but unto him* which died for them and rose again." (II Cor. 5:15).

Yielding to Christ means opening every part of the life to Christ, that He may fill it with Himself. Whatever we open the life to, that fills us. If I open my being in any measure to Satan, to the world and to the flesh, I am filled to that degree by them. But if I open every door to Christ, to the Spirit and to the Word, then they fill my mind, my heart, my spirit.

Yielding is not infilling, but it prepares for it. Emptying makes ready for infilling. Only the yielded life can be filled with the Holy Spirit. Have you yielded yourself to the Lord Jesus Christ?

How May The Fullness Be Obtained?

The way is so simple but man sometimes makes it so complex. Some think it requires long fastings, all nights in prayer, seeking with agonizing, constantly praying for the infilling but never receiving it, earnestly seeking but never finding it. In one institution where the message of the Spirit-filled life was given at a meeting of Christian workers, we were told afterwards that every week for a whole year they had prayed for the fullness of the Spirit but had not yet received this blessing. A missionary told me she had prayed every day for this fullness but had no answer. Then is God not willing or not able or not ready to bestow the fullness upon His children? Yet He commands them to be filled. In what an unreasonable, unkind position this places God.

What is God's way? It is so simple and so clearly stated. Listen to His words.

"Whosoever *drinketh* of the water that I shall give him" (John 4:14).

It is the active appropriation of a gift.

"Jesus cried, saying, If any man *thirst*, let him *come* unto me, and *drink*" (John 7:37).

Could anything be more simple? One does not have to get down a big lexicon or commentary to understand the meaning of one of these words. They are part of your everyday vocabulary. We miss the way because it is so simple.

"*Any man*"—there are no favorites with God. When God says "any man" it is as though He wrote in your own name there. Only it is far, far better just as it is. A few years ago I received a letter from a young girl who signed herself "Ruth Paxson." So if it read, "If Ruth Paxson thirsts" how would I know that it did not mean her instead of me? But when God says, "If any man" then it means the one who meets the conditions stated. And what are they?

"*Thirst*"—this is not mere desire for something I vaguely feel I ought to have which I do not possess, or a longing born of jealousy or envy possibly, for a power which is seen in some Spirit-filled life. Thirst is an intense desire for holiness for Christ's sake that must be satisfied. It is an intense craving for power to witness for Him and to win souls to Him that must be quenched. Nay, even more than this is enfolded in that word "thirst." It is an insatiable longing for God Himself. It is that inward heart cry of the Psalmist of old.

> "As the hart panteth after the water brooks,
> so *panteth my soul after thee*, O God. My
> soul *thirsteth for God*, for the living God"
> (Ps. 42:1, 2).

It was expressed in a letter received just yesterday here at Keswick, "I am unquenchably athirst for Him and His holiness." Do you have this kind of thirst? It is the first condition for obtaining the fullness. Then what?

"*Come.*" Where and to whom? To a "tarrying meeting?" To a conference, even Keswick? To some human leader? "Come unto Me"—the only One who can bestow this gift: the Giver of this living water in all its fullness. Have you come to Him? Perhaps you have come and *asked* for the gift. But that is not His condition. He states it clearly. The asking is bound up with the thirsting. But aspiration even expressed in asking is not enough. There is something more for us to do.

"Drink"—this is an act. Aspiration becomes acquisition by appropriation. Thirst is desire—I want water. To drink is an act—I take water. Just here is where many earnest, seeking souls fall short of this glorious experience. They thirst but they do not drink.

After a meeting where this message was given a very sad-faced woman stopped to shake hands and said, "Oh, Miss Paxson, I thirst!" I waited to hear the rest of our Lord's blessed invitation and to know she had acted upon it. But she went out still sad-faced. But she returned to the afternoon meeting where we went further into the way of obtaining this fullness. Again she stopped and with a radiant light in her face said, "Oh! I thirst and *I drink*." A letter came from

her later in which she said, "I keep on thirsting
and drinking and He keeps on satisfying."

In these words is the secret not only of obtaining the fullness of the Holy Spirit but of having
that fullness maintained continuously in the life.

"Be not drunk with wine
But be filled with the Spirit."

How does one get drunk? By drinking. How
does he stay drunk? By continuing to drink. How
is one filled with the Holy Spirit? Our Lord says
by drinking of that living water. How does one
stay filled? By continuing to drink day by day.
Is that not simple for each one of us in this tent?
May we bow in silence to face a few questions
in the presence of the Lord, and answer by a
definite "Yes" or "No."

Have you ever been filled with the Holy
Spirit?

Are you filled with the Spirit now?

Will you be filled today?

Do you purpose to live the Spirit-filled life
from now on?

If you thirst and will drink just now, will you offer to God this simple prayer: "Lord, I thirst; Lord, I come and drink; Lord, I take the gift Thou offerest, the fullness of the Holy Spirit, and thank Thee for it."

WRESTLERS FOR CHRIST

IV

WRESTLERS FOR CHRIST

That wonderful Epistle to the Ephesians, in which we have the highest truth regarding the mutual relationship between Christ and the Christian, is divided very naturally and easily into three parts, and it follows the divine order

The Wealth of the Christian.
The Walk of the Christian.
The Warfare of the Christian.

In the first three chapters we have a revelation of the riches of Christ, the riches of glory, the unsearchable riches of Jesus Christ. They are the possession of the one who is in Him. Then, beginning with verse 1, chapter 4, and on through to verse 9, chapter 6, we are given a revelation of the sevenfold walk of the Christian, who is to walk worthy of the high calling to which he has been called in Christ Jesus. It is in this part of the Epistle that we have the greatest of all commands in the New Testament for the Christian: "*Be ye filled with the Spirit*" — that experience of the Spirit-filled life, the greatest experience, the deepest experience that one can have this side of heaven.

The Call To Warfare.

One would almost think that that was the place to stop, but God does not think so. In verse 10, chapter 6 there is the word "Finally," and that word "finally" indicates not only the close, but *the climax* of the truth of this Epistle. The Christian is not through yet. It is not enough for him to luxuriate in the life that is his as a child of God, and an heir of God. It is not enough for him just to walk with the Lord worthily and consistently. The Christian has a task set before him, and that task is nothing short of warfare. When you enter into chapter 6 at verse 10 and go on to verse 12, you are immediately on the battlefield; and there is *a real warfare being waged*. Who is so prepared for the warfare as the one who has entered into the fullness of his inheritance in Christ, as the one who 's walking worthily and consistently with God, who has indeed been filled with the Holy Spirit? It is only such a one that God can trust to be a part of that great army under the Captain of the host, going forth into this terrific spiritual warfare. So it is inevitable that this Epistle to the Ephesians should end on a battlefield.

This week in Keswick we have heard messages revealing to us so clearly what are the unsearchable riches of Christ. I trust it means for every one of us that we have entered more fully and more perfectly into our inheritance in Christ Jesus, and that we shall go from this place infinitely richer in Him than when we came. I trust it means, too, that as we have heard these messages from God's Word pointing out to us what is the consistent, upright walk of the Christian, that we have begun to walk more worthily. Then we came up to Thursday, to that day of climax in a way, when in one message after another, the message of the Spirit-filled life, a life lived in the power of the Spirit, was presented in each successive gathering. The day ended with that glorious meeting where there were many who, for the first time, took the fullness of the Holy Spirit by faith, and others who had had that fullness, but had lost it, came again into that precious experience. Did Keswick end on Thursday night? By no means. On Friday and again yesterday there were set before us the great spiritual battlefields of the world, and the far-flung frontiers of the vast mission field. And we have just as big a battlefield here in the homeland; here also is a spiritual warfare going on. To whom will God look? To whom can He entrust this spiritual warfare? Is it not to us who have entered more fully into our wealth in Christ, who are going out to walk more worthy of Him? Are we prepared tonight to hear His call for spiritual wrestlers, spiritual warriors, for the great conflict of today and tomorrow? We have been witnesses for Him; we have been workers together with Him; but there is something even beyond that.

A few years ago in China I was asked to take a Bible class for young men in the professions.

I never like to assume a task like that without entering into some new, deeper experience in my own life. I am afraid of giving to others from out of stale manna. I always want some fresh, new touch of God upon my own life. So, as I took this Epistle to the Ephesians for that Bible teaching, I asked the Lord to give some new message to me, to make some new demands upon my own life. When I came to verse 12, chapter 6, the Lord gave it to me in that word "wrestle." "For we *wrestle* not against flesh and blood, but against principalities, against powers, against the rulers of the darkness of this world, against spiritual wickedness in high places." I said, Yes, that is a new call! I have been a witness; I have been a worker at home, and in the mission field, but never before have I had a call made to me to be a *spiritual wrestler.* Friends, I did not know then what it meant! I would have been cowardly had I known all that it meant to make the promise to God that I would be a spiritual wrestler. But I did promise, and I asked Him if He could trust me, that He would put me out in the front line, in the firing line, in the thickest of the fight. In these last few years He has let me know a little of what it means to be a spiritual wrestler in a real spiritual warfare.

This then is the message that He has given to me to bring to you tonight; simply to be His voice, making the last call to the people in this Keswick Convention that you will not be satisfied with being merely a witness, with being even a worker; but that you will offer yourself to God to be a spiritual wrestler, a spiritual warrior, with all that may be involved in a real spiritual conflict, for the victory in your home, in your church, in your community, in your country, and in this world, in these last days before the Lord comes.

Our Foe

Let us turn, therefore, to chapter 6 and so learn about this spiritual warfare, and all that it means, from God's own Word. "Finally, my brethren." Paul does not say, "my fellow apostles," or "my fellow commanders." No, he says, "My brethren." Paul is saying there, my fellow soldiers." No Christian is exempt from this warfare. God has no place for spiritual pacifists. He calls every saint to arms.

> "For our wrestling is not against flesh and blood, but *against principalities, against the powers, against the world rulers* of this darkness, *against the spiritual hosts of wickedness* in the heavenly places" (Eph. 6:12, R.V.).

The stage of the battle is set. We "*wrestle.*" It is an intense struggle; it is a hand to hand combat. We "wrestle *against*"—five times the word "against" is used. We have an out and out adversary; there is a fierce, aggressive, active, satanic opposition. Who in this tent has not felt it? Who of us has not met it in his own personal life, in his home, in his work? But we are so apt to think that this conflict is with flesh and blood; that it is with some person in our home with whom we find it almost impossible to live, although it may be a blood relation; you dread to go back again to that person tomorrow; it is a comfort to be away from that person even for a short time. It may be some missionary is here who is glad to be on furlough because he is not living any longer with that person he has had to live with! the furlough means partly getting away from that person for a time. Let us be honest. We have considered that our wrestling was with flesh and blood; and we have been fighting against the human element; and that is why we are defeated, and we have not won out. But "we wrestle not against flesh and blood," not against a human, visible foe, not against a foe that is our equal or one on the same plane with us. No, it is against a superhuman, invisible foe that we wrestle.

Satan—A Person

In this chapter there is revealed a distinct alignment between God and His hosts, and Satan and his hosts. Supernatural persons are pitted against each other. It is perfectly foolish for us to underestimate Satan's power. He is an actual, active, aggressive enemy. And this chapter reveals to us that he is the head of a host, organized, mobilized, and energized by himself. Our adversary is a supernatural person. What are some of his names? He is the deceiver, the devourer, the tempter, the accuser, a liar, a murderer. These names indicate his nature; they make us shiver with fear and recoil with loathing. All these names indicate what he is like. He seduces, he deceives. His work is destructive and diabolical; and this is our adversary.

Satan—His Position

As a supernatural person he occupies a superior position. Christ Himself three times spoke of him as "the prince of this world," with governmental authority over men. He is "the prince of the power of the air," with governmental authority over evil spirits. He is "the god of this world," with spiritual authority over men.

Satan—His Power

He is a person with supernatural power. The Bible does not deny it; it calls that supernatural power "the power of darkness." He is strong, powerful, and mighty. He is powerful in his methods, which are those of the gangsters of the underworld. He works by wiles, strategies, devices, and subtleties. The Bible says he is powerful in organization. He works through principalities, and powers, and hosts of wickedness. He is powerful in equipment; he has a stronghold, and armor, he has spoils, and goods. Our adversary is a supernatural person, occupying a superior position, and exercising supernatural power.

Satan—A Defeated Foe

It is foolish to underestimate the power of Satan, but *it is fatal to overestimate it.* There are people who talk too much about the devil, and too much about his power. He likes to hear us talk about his power. His power is mighty, but it is not almighty: he is powerful, but he is not all-powerful. He is an absolutely defeated foe. Christ is the Stronger Man, and He has bound the strong man, and has despoiled him of his goods. As the representative Man in the wilderness, He met the devil, and He won a decisive victory over him; and He won it in the only way in which you and I can win that same victory. He was led into the wilderness filled with the Holy Spirit; and the only weapon He had was the Word of God. Three times as He faced that tempter He said, "It is written!" And there is no man or woman in this tent who may not go back and gain the victory in that same way, filled with the Holy Spirit, and with the precious Word in the mind and in the heart, ready to be used in any moment of temptation. The devil can be a defeated foe for you and for me.

The death of Jesus Christ wrested from Satan every vestige of his claim upon mankind. Through the resurrection and the ascension He returned to His Father as Victor over Satan and all the forces of hell and of sin. He openly triumphed over all principalities and powers. Through His exaltation He was crowned by the Father, Lord of lords, and King of kings; Lord of the universe, and "Head over all things to the Church." Through His finished work Jesus Christ entered Satan's territory and won it back inch by inch for His Father. Satan was judged and sentenced and doomed when Jesus Christ died upon the Cross, but the sentence has not been fully executed, and will not be until Christ returns. So, in the meantime, he contests the Lord's victory, and he fights to retain sinners in his captivity, and to regain saints under his control.

This is where you and I come in in this warfare. When Jesus Christ was upon earth every attack was against that precious physical body of His, the body He took upon Him in order that He might lay it down in death upon the Cross as your Saviour and mine. He rose out of that tomb with that same body, but a spiritual body. He is today at the right hand of the Father in that body; He is there as the God-Man, as your High Priest and as mine. Now we are His mystical body; we are the only part of Christ that the devil can now touch; we are the visible part of Him on earth; that is why you and I come in in this awful warfare; your life and mine is a part of that battlefield on which this spiritual warfare is being conducted.

Satan—His Tactics

How does Satan work in this warfare? Our first necessity is to know *the enemy's position*; and the second, is to know *the enemy's tactics*.

"Put on the whole armor of God, that ye may be able to stand against the wiles of the devil" (Eph. 6:11).

We must understand Satan's objective. The Lord tells us what it is. He said to Peter, "Simon, Simon, Satan hath desired to have thee that he might sift thee as wheat." Satan is hell's head gangster. He is in this world seeking to steal that pearl of great price that belongs only to the Lord Jesus Christ; and every bit of his work is done as a gangster of the underworld, one whose work is done through deception and subtlety. There is no mean and despicable trick he will not employ. He revels in the torment of the saints. He bores his way through into your life and mine in order to get control of them. He comes in, mainly through our imaginations, our thoughts, our attitudes. He comes into that innermost part of our being so silently, and so subtly, that we hardly know it is he, and we hardly know he is there. Then once he is there he attempts to overthrow and overcome us by the invasion of a sudden temptation, and at a time when he is likely to find us unsuspecting and unprepared.

Notice that God does not tell us to put on that armor of His in order to stand against the strength of the devil, but in order to stand against the *wiles* of the devil. That is what you and I need to guard against—*the wiles of the devil.* How does he get in through these wiles? I want to mention a few of the ways in which he is working today in us personally.

Through Depression of Spirit

Oh, the number of saints today in whom the devil, not only has a place, but has control through depression! He brings to them doubts and discouragements regarding their spiritual condition. Whenever such doubts and discouragements assail you, you may know that it is of the devil. God never torments one of His children; and when this depression of spirit means torment and torture for you and me, we may know that it is the devil at work in our hearts. It is his mark.

All he wants is that we should get our eyes off of Christ. If he can do that through this concern as to our spiritual condition, he has won his first victory in your life and mine. He will lead us on to morbid introspection, and to a deadly dissection and analysis of our spiritual condition. It is fatal! The moment we find ourselves so doing we should be on our guard. Satan never asks for the control of your life and mine at the first. All he asks is for a place there. We have that command so simple and definite, "Neither give place to the devil." All he wants, first of all, in your life is standing room, and he knows if he can get standing room he will soon get control; and he can get that standing room through depression of spirit.

Through Delusion of Mind

The world is being flooded by organizations, and movements, and fellowships, many of them satanic in origin, many of them containing half-truths and half-lies, subtle counterfeits that deceive even the very elect. Satan today will take even that most glorious truth, the truth of the Holy Spirit, and he will use it, and capitalize it for himself. Thus through cunning deception Satan lays hold upon many hungry-hearted people, and leads them away from the Lord and His Word.

Through Distraction of Heart

There has never been a time of such universal distress upon the earth. Many of God's children have been caught in the vortex of it. The loss of position, money, or business; experiences of crushing sorrow; or unprecedented conditions, have so laid hold upon some and have brought such distraction of heart that people cannot even get their minds upon the Lord. I have had letters from people suffering from just this kind of distraction of heart.

Through Deflection of the Will

The supreme business of the Christian is to do the will of God. But what is God's will? That is the question that countless people are asking today. They are thoroughly distressed over matters of guidance. As a citizen, what is to be one's attitude toward world problems? There are things going on in the church that we cannot believe are according to the Word of God, or according to the standard set by Christ. As members of the church, what are we going to do? Are we to protest? Are we to stay in the church or not? There are problems on the mission field—the relation of the missionary to the Board; the relation of the missionary with his fellow workers; where, perhaps, there are two in the same station teaching exactly opposite things. A pastor's wife in China came to me and said, "What am I to tell the heathen women I am bringing to church Sunday by Sunday, when at one service one missionary preached on the deity of Christ, and the next Sunday a missionary living on the same compound denied the deity of Christ?" What shall that pastor's wife do? These are problems which are facing us today as never before. There are the problems connected with our social life. Here is a home where the Word of God is believed and taught; and the children go out into the school, and the university, and into society, and they are forced almost into things which are against the principles of those parents. What are the parents to do? Stand out against these things, or yield to these things that their children are having to face today as members of society? As members of society how can we keep unspotted from the world? So Satan tries to darken the mind, and to bring about discord.

Through Distress of Body

How many of God's saints are meeting real attacks from the evil one in the realm of the body.

Through Discord in the Home

Through alienation between husband and wife, parents and children; through misunderstanding between members of the same family.

Through Division in the Church

Yes, division in that part of the church that is sound and true and evangelical. It has been my privilege to travel in ten different countries in Europe. I am sorry to say it, but I have scarcely touched in any country any work that is absolutely sound and true and evangelical, that there is not somewhere at the heart of it, or within it, division that is caused by intolerance of workers one with another, by insignificant things, by jealousies. It is the devil's most deadly work within the evangelical part of the church of Jesus Christ.

These are some of the ways in which Satan is working today. They are enough to set before us the truth that we are in the midst of a spiritual warfare.

The Wrestler—Equipment for Warfare

What are we to do? We must admit the power of the adversary. He is bent on our undoing or overthrow. But need the Christian be fainthearted? Need he be overcome? No! He need not be defeated if he will take hold of these few verses in Ephesians 6, and do the things he is told to do there.

The Assurance of Power in Christ

We will think now of what is the Christian equipment for this warfare as revealed in these few verses. First, the assurance of power in Christ.

> "Be strong in the Lord and in the power of his might" (Eph. 6:10).

"*Be strong!*" That is what He is saying to us tonight. You will soon be returning to your homes. Oh, that these words might ring in your hearts, "*Be strong!*" What will the devil say to you? He will say, "Be fearful! Think of the dangers and difficulties ahead. Think of the home to which you have to return; the place of business; the social circle. Be cowardly! Give up, and turn back. Be weak! Sink under the weight of the circumstances of your environment. Be a deserter!" That is what he was—a deserter! Satan deserted God, and set up a kingdom of his own; and he will try to get you and me to be deserters.

The devil will try to get us to look back and to turn back. You say, I was moved at that meeting; but I am afraid it was all emotion. How the devil loves us to say that when some decision is made under the conviction of the Holy Spirit. In a moment when we are at our best—and it is only when we are at our best we should make our decisions—the devil will try to get us to say that it was all emotion. That will be the devil's voice to you; but the Lord is saying to you, "Be strong!"

Our strength, therefore, does not lie in outward armor, but in an inward attitude, in the assurance of our power in Christ. Do we enter the conflict assured of the power to win, or are we overcome with dread and fear before beginning? "Be strong *in the Lord!*" The Lord is more than a match for Satan. He has already bound the strong man; He already is Victor. Mark it so that you cannot help but see it constantly, that little word "in." "Be strong *in* the Lord!" That little word contains the whole secret of victory over the devil. It is where we are that determines our victory. *In Christ* we are more than conquerors. "Be strong *in* the Lord, and *in* the power of His might."

Our power is in a Person. Three times in the next few verses we read this word, "That ye may be *able to stand* against the wiles of the devil" (verse 2). "That ye may be *able to withstand* in the evil day" (verse 13). "Wherewith ye shall be *able to quench* all the fiery darts of the wicked" (verse 16). He is able, and we are strong in His power, and in the strength of His might. Mr. Raws, of the American Keswick Convention, has a little child who heard that hymn, "Onward,

Christian soldiers!" and the little three-year-old
was singing it, "Undone Christian soldiers!" That
is the trouble with most of us, we are undone
Christians, rather than Christians marching on
to victory all the time.

The Assertion of our Position in Christ

Secondly, our equipment for this warfare is
the assertion of our position in Christ. What
is our position in Christ? Where is He, and
where are we? Where is He? "Far above all
principality, and power, and might, and dominion.' That is where Christ is. Where are we?
Turn back to the second chapter,

> "And hath raised us up together, and made
> us sit together in heavenly places in Christ
> Jesus" (Eph. 2:6).

Why, if we had been made to stand together
with Him, it would have been wonderful. But
we are made to sit together with Him. And
when we sit we are relaxed: we are resting. And
we are seated together with Him in the heavenlies, "far above all principality, and power, and
might, and dominion." Is that divine rhetoric,
or is it divine reality? It is because this truth is

so precious to me that I glory in this privilege of passing it on. We will know constant victory if we will simply take our position in Christ, seated with Him in the heavenlies, "far above all principality, and power, and might, and dominion."

It does not tell us in Ephesians 6 to fight. That is the trouble. We are such fighters: we want to do the fighting; but it is Christ who does the fighting. All he asks of you and me is to stand in the victory that He has won, and is winning. Are you not tired of fighting? Then stop it; and do nothing but stand, unafraid, unmoved, undaunted, even before the devil and his hosts. We do not fight for a position of victory but from one. Therefore we may stand in Christ, reckoning the battle won before it is begun. In the very thick of the fight; in the darkest hour— stand. And what will happen? I like Weymouth's translation: "Stand your ground on the day of attack, and having fought to the end, come off victors in the field."

The Acceptance of our Protection in Christ

Then, our equipment for this warfare demands an acceptance of our protection in Christ.

> "Put on the whole armor of God, that ye
> may be able to stand against the wiles of
> the devil" (Eph. 6:11).

Paul knew much about soldiers; he was chained
to one when he wrote this Epistle. He probably
studied every part of that armor; he knew the
value of each part. The armor is for protection;
no part of the body must be exposed; even one
vulnerable part might mean defeat.

"The whole armor"—We cannot pick and
choose with this armor. We must put on the
whole armor; it is not intended for comfort or
convenience; and we are to wear it all the time.

"Of God"—It is the armor of God. What a
relief that is! We do not have to make it. How
little we know of Satan's strength and strategy!
and of our own cowardice and conceit! But God
knows all about him. and about us, and He pro-
vides the armor; and adapts that armor to the
nature and the necessity of the warfare.

"Put on"; "Take unto you"—We are to put
it on; it is not for show; it is for wear; it is for
use. And, friends, when once we have put on all
this armor it will not be very comfortable to sit

down in an easy armchair! If we are not willing to be in the thick of the fight do not let us put this armor on. Notice that there is only one part of the body that is unprotected—it is the back. God expects no deserters. There is no protection for the back. I do not want the enemy to be able to hit me in the back because I deserted my God in the time of trial, or affliction, or some dark hour in my life. God does not expect one of us to retreat, but to go steadily on as Spirit-filled overcomers.

God's Call for Wrestlers

We have asked many things of Him this week, and, oh, He has granted them so abundantly! We have received so much from Him. Now has He not a right to this last moment? Has He not now the right to make a request of you and me? He is asking you tonight through this precious bit of His Word if you will give yourself to Him as a spiritual wrestler. He wants you to leave Keswick longing to get back into the very thick of the fight, longing to get back to that difficult situation.

He is going to use you, perhaps, to win that soul that would mean the last one needed to complete the body of Jesus Christ, and so hasten His return. He is going to use you to go back and help some worldly, dissatisfied, defeated Christian to come into this blessed experience of the fullness of the Holy Spirit, that she too may be prepared for the coming of the Lord, if He should come tomorrow. This is God's call to you and to me tonight. It is the call for spiritual wrestlers, for spiritual warriors, who will go out into this warfare that must grow worse and worse as the time for our Lord's return draws nearer and nearer. I ask you now if you will, in the silence of this moment, say: "Yes, Lord, I give myself to Thee in some fresh new way! Thou hast asked for spiritual warriors. It is the Captain of the host who is asking for spiritual warriors. Lord, I respond! I give myself to Thee. And I ask Thee, if Thou canst trust me, to put me right out in the front firing-line, where the warfare is thickest." Will you say that to God? This is what He ought to have from us as a glad, joyous response for all that He has given to you and to me during the days of this week at Keswick.